T0380898

Moving is

Awful

Ty Hatcherson

To order additional copies of this book,
contact:
Xlibris
844-714-8691
www.Xlibris.com
Orders@Xlibris.com

ISBN: Softcover   979-8-3694-2499-5
         EBook   979-8-3694-2498-8

Print information available on the last page

Rev. date: 07/16/2024

Moving is Awful

At first, I was excited about moving to California.

I was excited about beaches.

I took beautiful photos
of my mom in Malibu.

I was amazed by
the mountains,

and the big, beautiful sun.

Then I got here,

and at school I was

the "new kid".

4th grade was quickly over, and summer was approaching.

I spent my summer
in Texas.

5th grade is here.

I am now the big
man on campus.

Everyone knows me
and you know what,
I discovered,

moving is not so
awful after all.

I have to admit,

I love LA.♥

Printed in the United States
by Baker & Taylor Publisher Services